a short history of crazy bone

a short history of crazy bone

long poem

patrick friesen

Mother Tongue Publishing Limited
Salt Spring Island, BC
Canada

MOTHER TONGUE PUBLISHING LIMITED
290 Fulford-Ganges Road, Salt Spring Island, B.C. V8K 2K6 Canada
www.mothertonguepublishing.com
Represented in North America by Heritage Group Distribution.

Copyright © 2015 Patrick Friesen. All Rights Reserved.
The use of any part of this publication reproduced, transmitted in any form or by any means, electronic, mechanical, photocopying, recording or otherwise, or stored in a retrieval system, without the prior written consent of the publisher—or, in case of photocopying or other reprographic copying, a licence from Access Copyright, the Canadian Copyright Licensing Agency, info@accesscopyright.ca—is an infringement of the copyright law.

Book Design by Marijke Friesen
Cover: *Trickster*, 2002, oil on canvas, 30" x 36", by Eva Wynand
Typefaces: Dante and Rougfhouse
Printed on Springhill Cream, 100% recycled, FSC certified
Printed and bound in Canada.

Mother Tongue Publishing gratefully acknowledges the assistance of the Province of British Columbia through the B.C. Arts Council and we acknowledge the support of the Canada Council for the Arts, which last year invested $157 million in writing and publishing throughout Canada. Nous remercions de son soutien le Conseil des Arts du Canada, qui a investi 157$ millions de dollars l'an dernier dans les lettres et l'édition à travers le Canada.

Library and Archives Canada Cataloguing in Publication

Friesen, Patrick, 1946–, author
    A short history of Crazy Bone / Patrick Friesen.

Poem.
ISBN 978-1-896949-49-9 (pbk.)

    I. Title.

PS8561.R496S56 2015   C811'.54   C2015-900390-3

*For Anna Sawatzky, Jacob Sawatzky
and Margaret Sawatzky Friesen*

1

All the rivers run into the sea . . .

Ecclesiastes 1:7

1

crazy bone is born
at the river

each time she meets it
and goes under

it takes a moment
that passes away

she lands a fish
with bare hands

crazy bone knows
where the still pools lie

*nothing still that I know
but what do I know?*

2

she listens to summer rain
among the poplar leaves

*there's a place
for a little child*

morning glories and peonies
along a weathered fence

she sings like someone
she once heard

the songs are old
of cradles shawls and longing

crazy bone hitches her skirt
and dances like the greek

there is tartar in her blood
there are horses in her dreams

3

crazy wakes
at the darkest hour

the dogs in town
have gone quiet

this is when
she dreams

*what arrives
in the dark?*

far off the radiance
of a phone booth

in her hands
the power of keys

*what arrives in time
and out of time?*

*and all the time
that time takes*

4

on dust and gravel roads
crazy walks around the town

*maybe the walls will fall
and the dead rise*

she turns to scratch her height
on a birch

*but you can't measure
the river*

for a long time
it's noon all day

crazy stands
in her shadow

then the sun sinks away
as she drinks her thirst

*what do you know
for maybe?*

*you lazy
rolling river*

5

crazy bone laughs
like a loon

she's not crazy
but she's lean

a song at dusk
is what she loves

she remembers how he smoked
players plain

the way he lit
a match on his buckle

and how he gazed at her
with want

a fugitive and a vagabond
on earth

6

she watches a storm arrive
surrounding the town

a glow in the black-haired sky
and dry thunder all around

distant neon lurid as fog
pestilent and clotted green

a water bucket shines
beside the cricket's rasp

grass swaying beneath the rolling
wheel of sky

in her pocket
are five stones

which she needs to return
to a forgotten river

7

*shit shit shit
shit on a stick*

crazy stubs her toe
in knee-deep grass

muttering
she sits down

*yeah oh yeah
that's one for the books*

crazy removes her shoe
to rub the toe

*some day my prince
will come*

she grins wryly
holding her shoe

*one day once sure
but shit*

8

crazy bone likes a drink
and sleeps in a thicket

she spits on her fingers
to clean her face

crazy opens her purse
to dump it out

she thinks at dusk
thinks in shadows

*how ugly yes how bitter
and how gorgeous all the same*

crazy bone corks the bottle
and settles to pee

9

a phone at her ear
and an empty hand

crazy calls the law
to report an absence in the night

the light of the booth
contains her body

somewhere out there
all the animals live

she quotes ecclesiastes 1:7
tells them where to go

crazy bone hangs up
and steps out

where will I find the voice
that crosses the river?

10

she throws a stone
across a ditch

and steps off the road
for a look

in the ditch two crows pick
at the entrails of a dead horse

where's the knight?
where's his shield?

and where are the dead
in their sunday clothes?

crazy claps her hands and laughs
as the birds rise heavily

bloody corbies and
their shadows

11

crazy waves her arms about
agitated by mosquitoes

she tugs sleeves
over her hands

*when something's gone
where is it?*

she slows and stops
and stands still

*you think someone's coming
so you wait*

like a flamenco dancer
she raises her arms

hands cross at the wrists
and her back straightens

*I will be found
I know that*

swinging her legs over the rail
crazy jumps a fence

she surprises a song sparrow
and lands lopsided

surprised herself
to hear a yellowhead

a throaty call of love
and a sudden flare

well blow me down
flat

nimble and flippant
crazy lights a cigarette

she remembers a punch-line
but not the joke

it's funny I remember
anything at all

13

it's been two miles or three
crazy pauses on a dusty road

she's not been this tired
in one or two hundred years

crazy's not had a thought
in more than a week

last night she painted her nails
or it could have been before

*you never know what comes
or what's long gone*

his hands were on her
and he laid her back

*well jesus christ
there's always a surprise*

like maria madalena
she walks into light

through the clearing
birch and oak all around

she sits on a worn bench
waiting for the fox or deer

love is my sin
and love is my all

crazy ties back her hair
with a length of twine

she hears breath everywhere
or hears something

and falls asleep
beneath the lazy sun

15

crazy bone dreams a daughter
and a daughter dreams her

born in the basement
of a broken house

the shallow of the pond
is thick with cattails

crazy hoists her bottle
and takes a slug

god bless the cradle
and god bless me

she kneels in grass
listening to red-winged blackbirds

and god bless the grief
of every day ever

or is that going
too far?

she wanders the fields
heading home

and pauses to watch rain
a mile away

home isn't ever anywhere
near

crazy crosses the ditch
climbing to the road

her dress flutters
as the air suddenly moves

barely the scarecrow
of me

rain angles in and shifts
and walks beside her

crazy spreads one arm into the rain
the other into sunlight

one foot in front of the other
like maria spelterini

17

crazy stares at a fox
standing at the edge of the clearing

this has nothing
to do with me

now right now
nothing

she sinks slowly
into the grass

this is how it is
always

the fox turns its head
to gaze at crazy

no one ever looked at me
like that

and is
gone

as words fall into her body
she trembles in her thin dress

stockings bunch at her ankles
she digs a sliver from her thumb

crazy shivers in a sudden rain
from a cloudless sky

maple leaves scatter
a red breeze across the horizon

a hawk rises from a fencepost
rising in a spiral gust

heaven it must be heaven
from where I come

or the other
way around

crazy bone rubs her hands
to warm her blood

her blue dress shimmers
in the lowering sun

crazy buries her purse
covering it with dirt

she tears her photographs
throws them to the wind

the sun is late
and almost brown

*lose your life to find it
and find it every day*

crazy swings on the rusty gate
in a farmer's field

she sits on a harrow
overgrown with tufted grass

a swallow flashes and disappears
beneath the barn's eaves

*and if nothing is found
get over it*

20

this country
this tired country

crazy stands among blackened trees
the smell of char still simmering

a house full
a hole full

and you cannot gather
a bowl full

she hears a bird
the eerie echo of its call

and no answering
no flitting no flight

the silver point of new grass
in a burned-out hollow

my country is
smoke

there is no yes
or no

crazy bone spins her parasol
and turns around

21

crazy crouches in the morning
like a chimpanzee

she smiles at the thought
and hoots

who could have known
who? hooting

like the bird of desolation
in a moonlit field

she remembers entrails
and a prophecy

crazy rising
on trembling shanks

like I'm in
natural geographic

me and my disposable
thumb

22

she rolls a tire down the road
rolls it into a field of clover

wiping sweat from her brow
crazy falls to her knees

rolling over and over
on her green sleeves

then standing to listen
to the bell in town

whoever came from there
isn't me

she gathers flowers and poses
like the ghost of a bride

the occasions of time
belong to no one

a wedding
in a field

a lonely drowning
in some river

23

in the middle of a clearing
she sits on a wooden chair

splitting peas
into the lap of her skirt

*I dreamed he lay
beside the tracks*

with a sleeve
she wipes her brow

*the one whose face
is lost to me*

blowing a perfect ring
she watches it fade away

*to be forgotten
is the kindest thing*

crazy looks at her bare hands
turns them over

*grandmother shelling peas
into an enamel bowl*

*that would be me
wouldn't it*

crazy carves a pumpkin
for a face

she combs her hair
in a hand mirror

light fading
over the fallow field

and a silhouette
against the western sky

like a dark bonfire
or a pirouette

like eustacia vye
on the heath

crazy wipes the blade
of her pocket knife

christ on a horse
lit a fire in me

25

she lights a fire
rising into the night

*like the old people
on unploughed fields*

*or those in caves
with their red hands*

*and illegitimacy
running in my blood*

she remembers nights
from some november

stones and kindling
and a fallen tree

*what it is about fire is
that nothing's left*

*except ashes piling up
time after time*

crazy lifts her eyes
to flecks of light

*and maybe
some stars*

*time time time
where's my place?*

crazy bone leaves a trail
through heathen grass

her dress darkens
with dew

she moves heavily
in a dream

pines emerge vaguely
from the mist

*before shepherds
and before their dogs*

crazy shudders
into the day

wild-haired
with memory

*I combed and I combed
and I combed*

crazy flings her arms
outstretched

she swivels slowly
to dry her skirts

*before before
it was before*

27

she finds a burned-out shack
with the roof caved in

spear grass rises between
the spokes of a bicycle

she steps through the doorway
into an empty house

there's always a door
in the rubble

her face framed by the window
crazy gazes out at the fat blue and white clouds

the rich are with us always
but the view keeps the rest of us going

she snorts when she laughs
swallows and laughs again

isn't that the be-all
and the end-all?

crazy touches the sill
and rubs charcoal around her eyes

could have been a real beauty
if I say so myself

she smears her lips black
with a forefinger

if that isn't skin-deep
well what is?

28

crazy watches a lopsided moon
drift through the sky like an egg

he was a beautiful sleeper
completely gone

the night is chilly
with frost on barbed wire

and brittle grass
underfoot

when the door opened
light from the hallway

fell on his face
without waking him

crazy scrunches up
like a fetus

her eyes close
and her fingers curl shut

I think maybe awake
in another world

fish and moonlight
and you know whatever

she walks slowly
through the graveyard

annual sow thistle
milkweed and monarchs

the stones blaze white
in the afternoon

a crow sharpening its beak
on one of them

others mulling
in the poplars

what's been done
is undone

crazy finds a broom
in a shed

and sweeps leaves
from a grave

what was left undone
is done

she stops to blow
on her hands

no two ways
about it

30

crazy bone picks a wild rose
sucks blood from her finger

she sits to gather
her thoughts

loving how wind moves
like a river in the grass

*smoke drifted above his head
and his sleeves were rolled*

she straightens her dress
palm on her belly

*and still I remain
a lover in captivity*

crazy picks the petals
one by one

eating
every third one

32

as she rises for the day
she leaves her smell in the grass

I was known once
that's for sure

the grass slowly
releasing her shape

but what remains
of the lowly and the high?

all that mating
to feed the earth

crazy disappears and appears
through thin drifts of mist

that endless
hunger

god eat
god

32

crazy aghast at the sky
the clear blue slate of it

how naked and all at once
it is

she falls back on her heels
staring like someone blind

who if I look
can see me?

crazy clears her throat
just to hear a sound

breaking the spell
if I could

she lifts the middle strand
of a barbed wire fence

looking for the great
escape

33

she comes across a vacant house
and a parisienne on blocks

the smell of turps
from a toppled can

and a wooden ladder
against the eaves

crazy pumps water
from the well

splashes her face
and slicks back her hair

to be loved to madness
someone said that

a cat disappears
into the shed

crazy sits on the swing
and swings

singing *this little*
light of mine

crazy tugs a red dress from the line
behind the abandoned house

I will wear this wedding
and I will marry

she lets her blue dress slide
to pool around her feet

naked in the sun
and dazed

I will marry nobody
and no one marry me

crazy picks wild flowers
to weave a headdress

with this crown
I marry myself

she slithers
into the red dress

ah look at me
in my wedding colors

I am thief
of the rainbow

I am anything
I was born to

arms raised
crazy dances like a flame

*making
my escape*

*me myself
and I*

35

crazy remembers
and recites the names of gods

*loki christ
and whatever*

*moloch greed
adonai and before*

she sits down
on a bale of hay

scratching her arm
till it bleeds

*the ones with the heads
of birds*

crazy punctures a tick
with her thumbnail

*grandmothers and
the grandfathers*

*and me sitting here
like an old crow*

36

a thin night
and long

the owl is near
and small bones everywhere

*long time
no see*

crazy listening
to cries

a still cedar
in slender light

*new moon is nothing
but a tease*

*lighting up
the slaughter*

like a wing a breeze
strokes her neck

crazy on her elbow
propped against a tree

*it's just like this
how love arrives*

*that great old
come on*

swinging the door
wide open

long time
no see

37

crazy bone finds a body
in the underbrush

dark feathers
in yellow grass

and now
that is a story

she covers the bird
with earth

I should say
in its late stage

all afternoon leaves flutter
and are still

but no one
to tell it

no one
who knows it

crazy takes off
her gloves

let me out
of this coat

38

she dips her feet
in the creek

a kingfisher hovers
and plummets

into the silver light
of minnows

*the sudden blue
of it*

*is the world is
everything before*

*the colour of
water*

crazy skips a stone
down the creek

*not a flaw
or nothing but*

*that would be me
too*

39

*listening for word
of another place*

crazy listens to a train
a mile into the night

she lies down
beneath her coat

*death untimely
and oh*

crazy remembers
a helpless dream

*waiting between stations
on their knees*

*night all around
old night*

40

she flips a dime
to watch it flash

so many suns
could make you laugh

the flare off the pond
blinds her for a moment

sun on the back
of my eyelids

or the paintings
at lascaux

crazy remembers a photo
tacked to her bedroom wall

a great black bull
and the sun

not to mention the crescent moon
on the outhouse door

crazy bone stands aside
for a procession

the long black hearse
shining like a mare

raising dust
along town line road

*and me running barefoot
long ago*

a hearse two cars
and a pickup truck

*just time and
how it stretched*

*one loses a life
the other gains it*

crazy turns into the ditch
looking for bottles

*one of us
needs a drink*

chortling and clapping her hands
crazy bone rejoices

*as the dust rises
in a whirlwind*

*and returns
to rise again*

crazy runs around the clearing
kicking off her shoes

a deer startles from a thicket
and hightails it into the trees

breathlessly crazy slows
stops and sinks to the ground

*it's not the first time
no no not the last*

*bless my mother's womb
and bless the world's*

crazy coughs from laughing
and laughs again

*who would have
thunk it?*

43

whistling a tune
to fill the night

*feeling scattered
like the stars*

she walks slowly
in the dark

her hands before her
to feel her way

*the living can not be risen
before they're dead*

crazy stands still
to listen

*colonel bogey's march
I used to know the words*

44

she retrieves a fallen mirror
and cleans it with her sleeve

looking for a face
the one before before before

these fields in my face
and the face of the fields

it looks like someone
I once knew

she slants the mirror
to catch the sun

but then I'm not so sure
about that anymore

when a small fire catches
she pockets the mirror

putting away
a child's thing

she fans the fire
with her breath

somewhere and soon
there are no words

45

through a tunnel of bur oak
she slips along a path

into a field of wind
and void

*this must be something
like the other side*

*that door
we never open*

crows and thunderclaps
and a clear sky

*well I doubt it
I very much doubt it*

*but holy shit
I could be dead wrong*

keys to the cemetery
in her hand

*this is going too far
make no bones about it*

crazy bone balances on her toes
reaching for a plum

*what the rain offers
and the heat fattens*

cupping it in her hand
she licks off the dust

it glows royal purple
as she holds it high

*something
will die*

*for this to become
spirit*

juice drools
from her mouth

crazy spits the stone
and wipes her lips

*it's a honeymoon
and me near drunk*

47

crazy bone closes her eyes to pray
a slice of bread in her lap

for what I am
about to receive

one eye squints
open

from above
and below

crazy opens her bottle
and takes a long pull

she raises the bottle
to gaze at it

the spirit in me
is the spirit in you

crazy laughs standing
to take a bow

fire and water
water and fire

and earth
and smoke

yadda
yadda yadda

48

she cajoles a dog
growling in the ditch

an empty mountain dew
and purple loosestrife

bending forward
she reaches with a trembling hand

here boy c'mon boy
nothing to fear

I could be
your better half

her shoes are wet
and falling apart

crazy ruffles his fur
and kisses his snout

nothing to want
I smell his life

he licks her hand
then runs off

just a scent
left behind

49

branch to branch
crazy climbs a tree

birds and leaves around her
and the green glimmer of light

*there is a woman
then there isn't*

she clambers to a higher branch
her shoes dropping to the ground

*like she never was
and no one was*

crazy shoves leaves aside
to see the sky

*oh for the love of the lord
god feral*

*and me myself
and my country senses*

50

*the river has a mouth
and I have ears*

crazy bone draws her shawl
around her shoulders

she stands by the water
of approaching winter

a broken willow
dipping into the narrow seine

she's found an icy moon
in the late afternoon

*it is pleasing to me
the end as the beginning*

one hand filled
with stones

crazy calls across the river
her other hand rising to her mouth

2

...from whence the rivers come,
thither they return again

Ecclesiastes 1:7

52

naugehyde blisters
that july

top ten
on the radio

not one of them
my favorite

but I loved
my heels

though they took me
down the wrong street

all the way
to lourdes

and half way
back again

ran into christ
at the back door

just loitering
you know?

52

what can you say
when you hardly remember?

he danced me
into his car

and we drank and talked
until our clothes fell off

crazy raises her arms
to the sky

she gazes at her palms
to see her life

he smoked players
and he did me in

a train rolling
in the distance

and the distance
rolling in

that car drove us
across the world

and when the door opened
the rain came in

53

snow falls steadily
among the pine and birch

branches bowing
beneath the growing weight

a stillness brought
into the world

crazy strips an orange
peels bright on the snow

*my belly was round
and my breasts full*

she holds the orange up
to measure it against the absent sun

*I had a twin
that was me*

*and I nursed her
till my nipples cracked*

*I left her in the garden
to find the dance hall*

crazy segments the orange
and puts two aside

*when she became a child
I became a child*

smell of orange and
the scent of pine

crazy steps from
behind an oak

and hiding
I was hidden

only lies
could find me

54

jays are screaming
at crazy bone

she skedaddles away
from their swooping

they think they own
this ground

crazy squats behind a tree
and counts her blessings

no one owns
no ground

she squawks like a jay
remembering the car

and that door
showed me the way

the radio playing country
he threw me out

flat-out in the ditch
swallowing rain

red tail lights disappearing
in the night

the parisienne running
on fumes

55

sun sets at the end of a storm
spreading like a rose

*silhouettes vanished
as the sun went down*

bonfires on the horizon
fireflies glimmering in the dark

grass rustles and the
muscle of wings

*that night of pillage
arrived from god's eye*

*whatever
that means*

*leaving me naked
and a stone*

*beneath the oak rising
toward desolation*

*and who am I
to speak of it*

*with nothing
in me*

56

*all the photos buried
like seeds or stars*

*the shadows of them
and the light*

*like forgetting stories
all winter*

*the long winter
of burials*

*and who knows what
comes up in april*

a fox slips
into its den

leaving nothing
but a smell

and the thought
of an absence

*they are all dead
awaiting resurrection*

*in the other world
and in this*

57

a rusting corvair
and a broken rocking chair

a pair of blue scissors
among the daffodils

*a junkyard in history
or something like that*

*a rubbish heap
for my birth*

gizzards and bulging
fish eyes

a dusty rose columbine
and a mourning dove

*christ is the question
but no one's asking*

*no one's asking anything
and nothing is wild*

*that inside blade
you know?*

58

birch are almost invisible
against the fields of snow

bird tracks littered
around a mulberry

*this is the white page
the old ones said*

*this is where
we learn to read*

*and where language
melts away*

crazy on her knees
makes prints with her hands

*like grauman's
I should be in movies*

*me and
meryl streep*

*I was thinking
of something like freedom*

*jack rabbits owls
and blood*

she sweeps snow from a broken chair
with her bare hand

she balances on its three legs
by leaning forward

her hand
to her chin

*like the thinker you'd think
rodin in a trance*

*but nothing left
to think*

59

*dreams have been leaping
between now and then*

*and then goes both ways
if you think of it*

*an elegant boatman
poling the raft*

*like that old poet
impossibly tall with her white swan cane*

*and I never dreamed her
though she was in my dreams*

*who was she?
from some beautiful world*

*and now and now
well that was then*

*and it will be then
when the raft rides ashore*

*those swans gliding
away*

though I am scorned
I will be born again

they said dancing led to pregnancy
they were right

I have given birth
a thousand times

shame on you
they said

and I ate their shame
shamelessly

crazy raises her arms
and spins on her toes

I am not fooled by god
I am becoming mother

she dances around an oak
her breath going ragged

crazy's face shifts
into a gargoyle

she blurts a curse
and falls to earth

61

if I die
that's a big if

if I die
and when

and that's an if
as well

crazy bone sees a shine
on the road's shoulder

she bends
to pick up a quarter

I buy and sell nothing
I have drunk my greed away

she flips the coin
calls it tails

another win
win situation

and winning
I lose

sidearmed she throws the coin
skipping down the road

62

*at night
the ghosts of geese*

*white bellied
and flying low*

*me pale
as a gibbous moon*

*thinking clear and
not thinking at all*

*the smell of me
is the smell of god*

*and then nothing
in the sky*

*not even the sound
of wings*

63

yesterday I was a sparrow
falling to earth

today I am
a miró tadpole

crazy takes off her shoes
and hangs them around her neck

she walks into the stream
holding her skirt to her waist

her shawl slides into the water
and the current takes it

like an irish maiden
with seaweed clinging to my thighs

and all the milleniums
just pass away

like slippery silver fish
gliding by my ankles

her knife bloody
from trimming beets

her hands red
juice running down her wrists

*I am reddled
and watcher of these fields*

*I have a longing for the city
that gathering of the wretched*

*home of a million
anxieties and elations*

crazy licks her fingers
and smears her lips red

she pretends to raise a fork
to her mouth

and pretends
to eat

crazy wipes her mouth
and leaves

she finds a footpath
that twists up a slight rise

walking into late light
crazy stands a silhouette

she turns around
and turns again

*there's no leaving this place
no matter how far I walk*

65

good morning captain
good morning to you sun

rising in her red dress
crazy raises her arms

where's the waterboy?
where's the word?

the sun angles
through a perfect web

a fat spider glittering
golden at the core

the word is good
the word is good god

and the word is lucid
the word is lucifer

her hands shape a camera
and snap a photograph

holy holy shit
this will be a day for sailors

a day for sailors' songs
oh shenandoah

not a day for mirrors
no need to comb my hair

I shall comb the leaves
of the weeping birch

66

crazy reaches the end
of a path

she stops to gaze
across a clearing

the shadows of trees
grow longer

*standing here
like the god of all time*

*well maybe not
quite that*

*servant of thunder
slave of this place*

*something
high and mighty*

*me and the gods
nose to nose*

*and who can say
whatever*

*an owl with
a bone to pick*

*a blackbird
with its grievous wound*

67

crazy bone calls for a hawk
and soon a red-tail descends

she emits a high wild sound
singing from her throat

*the keys to the kingdom
but where's the lock?*

*and the secret is a secret
what do you expect?*

*but I have picked locks
and found myself captive*

crazy looks up squinting
her hand against the sun

*all things pass they say
but some things never come*

the hawk circles wider and
climbs the sky in a slow spiral

*disappearing isn't it
through my eye*

68

crazy is removing her clothes
one by one

oh me oh my
wired to high heaven

some days some of these days
it's hard to live

animal tracks running
through my blood

and electrical storms
in my brain

for christ's sake
always tending the fire

you know what I mean?
blowing on the embers

a born ranter
a raconteur deluxe

and though not yet godlike
I can show you my peach

she stands in her white slip
letting it slide

disobedience is the root
of wit

and witlessness is
the root of goodness

remember the joke
about the crack of dawn?

the rosy fingered
crack of dawn

*it was
in barcelona*

*some small square
near a cathedral*

*they danced flamenco
all afternoon*

*a music
no one heard*

*this skinny blonde
in a shining orange dress*

*leaning against
a stone wall*

*her head tilted
gazing at her partner*

*on his knees
weeping*

*I think the music
ran out*

*or the batteries
in his boom box*

70

there are sailors in the bush
waiting for their ships

though it's been a dry summer
and the sails have gone up in flames

land ho means nothing here
they are waiting for the sea's return

the clay is cracked
you can feel earth's breath

rhubarb leans over limp
as elephant ears

maybe I will find the sailors
and sew them new sails

they will tell me stories
of the stars

lorelei and the boatman
silkies and sirens

or I will bury them
beneath their oars

71

crazy climbs an oak
to a broken tree house

nothing but sky
and leaves

and a crow somewhere
in this tree

from here I could kill
the world

a poultice and
a prayer

she spots a hammer
at the foot of the tree

and clambers down
to look around for nails

nothing here but rust
and rope

crazy stops to chew
a splinter from her thumb

am I the nail
to repair this house?

72

waking up abrupt
she is barking sick

crazy shivers
in her thin dress

and with cold hands
puts on more layers

her fever rising
she begins to see things

as they are
as they most certainly are

*three-headed gods and
blind and crazy ones*

*and not one to help me
with my hallucination*

*those goddamned dogs
they sic on me for fun*

*that howling idiocy
of heaven*

73

walking toward nothing
as usual

and always getting there
for sure

as long as there's no one
and nothing to say

just oh shit
when I stub my toe

caught in a swift
shadow

and then sun
again

and me with time
on my hands

should I say nothing
but time?

74

she stops
at a crossroad

in the distance
a figure approaches

*who the hell
and what?*

*there's no getting
away from it*

*well when you can't be alone
you're probably not*

the figure disappears
in a dip

then appears suddenly
a lot closer

*christ in a nut shell
a mirage*

*it's a hunchback
or a child*

*oh look
will you look?*

*a child's face
and what a smile*

*like a sliver of glass
in my heart*

75

crazy finds a letter
in a ditch

and someone's walking
toward her

well if it isn't
rush hour

she looks at
the smeared envelope

like casterbridge
or tess or one of those books

and everything's going
to go wrong

she throws the soggy letter back
among the reeds

thinking about everything
that might have happened

the wind
could have taken it

or taken me
like it's done

the road is empty
the sky too

the ploughman
has no sowing

76

one foot jiggling
I was listening to the radio

listening to drunken notes
from a piano

that growly voice
with his hammered klavier

remembering a parade
in seville

with its crosses
and christ held high

remembering a brilliant
snow-lit night

and further back
where the seasons run together

my grandparents
ten thousand years ago

them walking across
the world

always moving always
on their way to water

and water always
on its way

77

*wishing for
some yoruba diviner*

*anyone
to guide me back*

*to the idea
of my life*

*some dream
in some cave*

*some cave
in some mind*

crazy taps her head
and smiles

*there is an animal
in my brain*

*and some days I go cold
as a rattler*

she looks back
over her shoulder

*but where is love
when you need it?*

*if it's anything
you need at all*

78

*well if it isn't the end of me
and harvest around the corner*

*that fat orange moon rolling
toward me like a cannon ball*

*tomorrow the scythe
and everything laid out golden*

*crazy pulls out her bottle
and salutes the moon*

*in the dark I wonder
who I am*

*in the light
I wonder the same thing*

*but it's all a stupid
wonder*

*spirit inside spirit
inside spirit*

*I knew a drunkard once
who blessed me*

79

from the edge of a clearing
she watches a man standing in the field

he doesn't move
just his hair in the breeze

the afternoon wears away
to the horizon's glow

him standing there like a mystery
like lot stood stone still

like some astonishing god
from a golden age

or a silent troubadour
in medieval times

he must have something
to say

he turns suddenly
and stares at crazy

whoa right through me
like a prayer

80

how do I know god
when I don't believe?

well I don't know god
anymore than god knows me

and that's backwards
like some lennon song

backwards like
reading mirrors

but I know of thee
ah yes with red wings in the marsh

I know of thee
and ambrosia

and maybe the secret
is in the dance

you know whirling about
until you think you're seeing things

that eye
inside the eye

ha that would be
me

or someone
probably someone

81

nature holds it
snot and spit and

holds the broken chair
and baby carriage

holds well pretty much
everything

grows it or
buries it

settles it all
in a long sleep

crows in their roost
fox in its den

but if I may be so bold
what is nature?

82

*those days on roslyn road
that was a city*

*an honest city and
blessed with music*

*from transistors from
the shoe shine door*

*all over osborne
and river avenue*

*me walking a balcony rail
seven floors up*

*as if I couldn't die
though I wanted to*

*and lit by sunset
above the elms*

*abendrot that kind of red
that kind of spreading rose*

*and someone spinning
records inside the apartment*

*that singing sparrow
that small singing sparrow*

*plummeting to earth
as she sang*

83

those wild cars thrashing
down country roads

dust raised to the height of trees
the cars small silver flashes

and those cars and boozing boys
and the slippery girls are all wild

that drunken ukrainian dance
with fiddles and guitars

and the lutherans and catholics
square-dancing into a hazy memory

swing your partner he calls
swing them round and round

some step out of the barn exhausted
howling among the moonlit poplar trees

crazy lights a cigarette
smoke a halo around her head

and this is the time for knocking
you know knocking at the door

and loose-hinged doors swing open
the cars rocking in the parking lot

and I squirmed on that leather seat
still sticky from the day's sun

spread and pinned like a butterfly
to a moment of my life

that was then and
this is then

though many winters
have come between

84

crazy bone gapes astonished
as a pickerel falls from the sky

well I guess
the one that got away

she smacks it on a stump
and guts it quick

her hands red
with entrails

she stands up
straightens her back

crazy pushes a stray hair
with the back of her hand

so there's a fish
where's the loaf?

85

mirror my mother said
look in the mirror and comb your hair

on her knees
crazy gazes into the river

listen I can whistle mozart
something churchy

or plunk piano keys
like schubert in that hotel bar

window mirror
on the wall

and those bulls those hidden
unbelievable bulls

crazy splashes her face
then stands up slowly

I am becoming old
becoming something or other

funny how old is always ahead
even though it's been

passing through the gateway
with its hunger

but sometimes
there's no going further

the gate groping
on its hinge

86

crazy makes a fist
then unfolds it

*look at my monkey hands
all the lines and wrinkles*

*a lot of memory
a lot of*

she looks at her hands
turning them over

*and here she taps her head
there are free thoughts*

crazy watches light grow dim
and night moving in

*there's no cockatoo on my shoulder
though there might as well be*

she gathers a few sticks
for a fire

*there are thoughts crazy
with color and shape*

crazy turns to hear coyotes
wailing in the distance

*ah they're hungry
or are they free?*

87

oh that was much later
a different man on a different day

he was younger
and came from another place

crazy sits down
to roll a cigarette

roll me a fatty I said
he took it for something else

later we smoked one
as we watched the moon

she looks skyward
and exhales in a long sigh

I'd have to say
my appetite came back

88

crazy jumps up
to stand on a tree stump

I guess I've earned
my life

you could say it is
a river of shattered glass

light everywhere and
nowhere

or maybe
whatever

she loses her balance
stumbles and falls

ha not much
of a stump speaker

and my sermon
unmounted

she makes
a sweeping bow

and now
for my next number

blah blah blah
blah blah blah

89

crazy sits in a rowboat
tied to a reed

*land ho he sang
with his fist full of bills*

*and me singing songs
of liberty*

*a breeze stirring
the water*

*and sun refracting
into pieces*

*I never read a book
about barcelona*

*but I knew it
like I'd forgotten it*

*and this is the leakiest boat
I've ever rid*

*just too much time
spent on the land*

*but I'll go sailing
in a song named after me*

*where the sailor drowns
underneath his hat*

crazy takes a loud bite
from a granny smith

*neither food nor thought
but both*

*there are things
neither true nor false*

*things that float between
or hover above*

*there are trains
that come and go*

*and there are bandits
who blow up the tracks*

*I'd like to build a little house
to set on fire*

*a white curtain fluttering
from a window*

92

she holds a lemon
in one hand

in the other
an open knife

*what's a little theft
here and there?*

*I have run out
of cuisine*

*just this taste
of some heaven*

crazy drizzles juice
onto her tongue

her eyes squinting
she grins

*living in this place
where it never rains*

*a refugee from
seville*

*or some dream
like that*

92

I am not here
to buy or sell

not here to eat
all things

remind me
of something true

let's say the bulls
in the caves

or the sea
turned red

or a bonfire
in the night

remind me
how they used to pray

how they were
serious

crazy pauses
and opens her hands

well
not too serious

she backs away
down the road

coming and
going

93

*but I grow wintry
in my thoughts*

*and love begins
to fade away*

*and so does me
me me*

*my stained hands
and mouth*

*my long-stained
dress*

*there will be no obituary
in port au spain*

*nor in montreal
nor in this neck of the woods*

94

I remember and
so I am

the afternoon
I almost drowned

the taste of
sunlit water

which I wouldn't remember
would I if I'd died

all the lies
and maybes

and there are lies
that hold fire

cold facts
I don't recall

she gestures dismissively
with her hand

who isn't in a story
now and then?

95

hear that wind
craving for tears

through spruce
and crooked jack pine

it's a long wind
in waves

an ocean yearning
for land or

the other way
around or

some other way
I haven't thought of

but there are tears
in the offing

that's one thing
sure

but whose or why
one can't tell

they say history
will know

but history doesn't know
what it knows

96

in mid-clearing
crazy bone stops

*now I know
the man in the field*

*that babylonian
ezekiel*

*waiting for the city
to burn*

*and me not having
a word to say*

*I would have laughed
if I'd known*

*his hair wild
as beard grass*

*some local yokel
with ideas*

she taps her head
and laughs

97

crazy bone builds a fire
like a ritual

gathering
wood and spark

for tinder
handfuls of dead leaves

in the womb
of christ

the growing
fire

what the preachers
don't know

everything true remains
hidden

you know?
what the hell

she shapes the fire
like a temple

or a tipi
you know?

a dwelling
for fire

98

crazy is looking into
her hand mirror

crows-feet
at the corners of her eyes

*I think I'm running
out of mirrors*

*what I see I
won't see anymore*

she goes down
on her knees

and scrapes a hole
in the dirt

she lays the mirror down
covering it up

*like everything
I've ever buried*

*every seed
and body*

crazy searches
in her pocket

*and I don't need to comb
my hair anymore*

*I'm too beautiful
for that*

she breaks the comb
in half

*I think maybe
I'm in 7th heaven*

99

crazy is walking sideways
through the trees

*like slipping
through a keyhole*

she stops at the edge
of a clearing

*I dreamed god
now by god I am dreamed*

*just me myself
and my carcass*

crazy stands still
gazing across the field

*spanish horses and me
sabotaging my life*

*always looking
for another*

100

she stops beside
spilled blood

*I wonder
what grew here*

*a slaughtered bull
and salvation*

*who would believe that
anyway?*

*half the time
I don't know anything*

*and half the time
I know less than that*

she stoops to smell
the blood

pokes her finger into it
and licks it

*all the time
I know everything*

*like an angel
coming down*

*the child dying
into this world*

crazy throws
her arms up

oh christ
what a lovely mess

101

*what is needed
can be stolen*

*gods are brought down
from high places*

*a horse blanket
a warm stable*

*and a pocketful
of rose hips*

*holding two thoughts
I cannot pull apart*

*and a third thought
having nothing to do with gods*

*when I wake I'll wash
my face in the river*

*and if by chance
I tell the truth*

*well
the joke's on me*

*and a grave is
a grave*

*my third thought
perhaps*

every third
thought

and me
just thin and bones

102

I heard a child
singing all night

arriving and fading
with the wind

but yet I do not know
my own breath

I know only
the owl

and its
plunder

the horse
unbridled

I know the trout
and the river

and beneath
the sun

the days of grass
swaying

and the child singing
among the leaves

1 0 3

a bone juts out from earth
crazy kicks it free

all the bones
that have been dug up

and the more
that have not been found

she brushes dirt
off the bone

cattle too are human
don't you think?

crazy waves the bone
like a talisman

I was in the cave
and I am here

isn't that
the truth

tattered and
scattered

she wraps the bone
and returns it to earth

someone said ask
and it will be given

that's never worked
for me

but trouble
I have always found

I've not sung
with the sweet anodynes

to err is divine
I said that

104

*lolling like
a lollard*

*a mumbling sister
to the dead*

*whatever I am
I've been*

*the many dead
I've buried*

*that unearthly city
the earth of us all*

crazy stops
and stands

*well I give
a rip*

I'd like to acknowledge all the tricksters in my family, past and present, Eva Wynand for the splendid painting which became the cover, Marijke Friesen for the book design, Mona Fertig and Mother Tongue, Niko, P. K. Brask, and always, Eve Joseph.